A Course in Basic Red Tantric Ritual Magic

Introduction

Although not widely understood, Tantra is a complete system of Pagan spirituality that utilizes yogic and occult methods to harness and use the energies of human sexuality for the purpose of the spiritual evolution of human consciousness, a part of which involves magical techniques for manifesting intentions ritually using various types of sexual activity, together with mantras, visualization techniques, pranic manipulations, and the deliberate creation of thoughtforms, artificial elementals, and akashic volts.

Although tantric practices are often experienced as blissful, eroticism is not the primary purpose of Tantra. The ultimate tantric goal is God-Realization; that is, actually becoming a god or goddess while still living in your physical body, and ultimately becoming a Sovereign in the Macrocosm (in the Hermetic sense), with perfect and balanced integration of masculine and feminine energies within your total being.

Thus, Tantra is closely associated with the techniques of Taoist spiritual alchemy, and particularly with the Magnum Opus working, otherwise known as "achieving immortality" by so transforming your soul to become a divine being who can prolong the life of the physical body indefinitely, and who is no longer required to endure compulsory physical reincarnation.

A true Tantrika who has successfully completed the Magnum

Opus becomes immortal while still in the flesh - sickness and disease no longer affect the health of the mind or body, wounds and injuries are healed almost instantaneously, and the life of the physical body can be prolonged indefinitely - even for thousands of years, if so desired. But those who attain this level of spirituality rarely choose to prolong physical incarnation, because their personal realization of the Godhead motivates them to serve humanity from higher planes of existence.

Tantric practices are often classified as being either White Tantra (the Right-Hand Path) or Red Tantra (the Left-Hand Path), the latter of which is, unfortunately, often associated with negative connotations by some practitioners and commentators. Generally speaking, the reason given for such negative associations is that Red Tantra involves engaging in a variety of sexual activities and magical practices without regard for judeo-christian concepts of ethics and morality.

That God created humanity with free will, and that He desires for us to exercise it, shall not be disputed; hence, the viewpoints expressed in this course are exclusively Pagan, and view judeo-christian concepts of spirituality to be both false and spiritually harmful to those who practice them. This course is devoted entirely, and only, to Left-Hand Path Red Tantric Ritual Magic and related practices.

The fundamental concept of Red Tantric Ritual Magic is the manifestation of any desire via the creation of a spiritual seed on higher, non-physical planes of reality, using human sexual energy. Once this spiritual seed, or "Magickal Child", has been created, it is subsequently and repeatedly energized by the performance of additional tantric rituals until it manifests as desired.

Of course, the manifestation of desires is often complex and subject to multiple constraints, such as:

Does the desired manifestation conflict with the desires of any other beings, many of whom are capable of blocking the attempted manifestations of other beings?

How much opposition exists toward the desired manifestation, in terms of its potential effects upon other beings?

What concatenations of events must occur on both physical and non-physical planes in order to manifest the desire; that is, how much work is really involved in making the desired manifestation a reality?

What are the implications of the desired manifestation upon one's personal destiny, and, more universally, upon the Web of Wyrd?

What, if any, are the potential consequences of successfully manifesting the desire, and are you ready, able, and willing to confront them?

With the above-mentioned considerations in mind, this author suggests careful deliberation upon all aspects of the desired manifestation prior to making a decision regarding whether or not to proceed to work toward manifesting the desire.

If, after careful deliberation, one decides to work toward

manifesting the desire, Red Tantric Ritual Magic, properly practiced, proves itself time and again to be one of the most rapid techniques of manifestation. Only very special mantric vibrations, and kabbalistic quadripolar utterances, can be deemed superior to Red Tantric Ritual Magic as manifestation techniques.

However, successful manifestations via mantras and kabbalistic utterance are advanced techniques, well beyond the abilities of practitioners who lack advanced occult knowledge, experience, and training. Men and women who lack such advanced training can, however, avail themselves of tantric techniques to manifest desires without having to endure long years (or even lifetimes!) of training.

Almost any type of sexual activity that culminates in orgasm can be utilized to generate sexual energy for the purpose of tantric ritual manifestation. Masturbation is effective for solo practitioners, and any type of sexual activity between two or more consenting adults (all male, all female, or both genders) is also effective. That said, the best results are generally obtained by one man and one woman working together, or by groups of male/female couples. This assertion is in no way prejudicial against homosexual sex magic; in fact, homosexual sex magic often obtains superior results over heterosexual sex magic, if the practitioners are knowledgeable and experienced. Even so, the Cosmic Principle of Duality ensures that male/female couples most often obtain the best results via tantric sex magic practices.

A multitude of books describing sex magic practices are currently available online, and this course makes no effort to judge or preempt any of them. Rather, the purpose of this course is to educate the general public regarding the true Pagan nature of Red Tantric Ritual Magic, and to describe the basic essence of its practice in terms that can be both easily understood and practiced by like-minded folks who have little or no formal training.

With these things in mind, the basic formula for manifesting a desire via tantric sex magic is:

1). Create a formal written statement exactly describing the desired manifestation in words, in any written language;

2). Create a unique symbol representing the desired manifestation, and then draw this same symbol on two separate pieces of paper;

3). Energize the symbol by engaging in slow, prolonged sexual activity while visualizing the symbol superimposed over mental images of the desired outcome, thinking and feeling all the while as though the desire HAS ALREADY MANIFESTED;

4). Anoint the paper symbols with all sexual fluids after orgasm (for couples and groups, orgasms need not occur simultaneously), and then store the paper symbols in a safe place until they are to be re-energized or disposed of (once manifestation has occurred).

These are the rudiments. Advanced practitioners may choose to incorporate additional elements into their practice, such as the conscious manipulation of pranic energy through their energy bodies to increase the amount of energy available for the manifestation, the vibration of mantras, the use of fluid condensers, the timing of rituals via astrological elections, etc.

Creating a Formal Written Statement of Intent

Prior to manifesting any desire, you must know exactly what you want, and you must express your desire in exact language, as simply as possible. This is more difficult than it may seem, because magical energies always seek the path of least resistance, and they do so quite literally. For example, if you desire to obtain a large sum of money, you may at first formulate a statement of intent such as:

I WILL GET A LOT OF MONEY

But this sentence has two major flaws: first, it is phrased in the future tense, and second, it does not specify how or when the money will be obtained. Therefore, if you use this sentence to create a magical sigil and then energize the sigil to manifest this desire, it may so happen that someone you love very much will be killed in an automobile accident next year, and you will inherit a large sum of money as a result of this unfortunate incident … probably not what you really had in mind!

A better statement of this intent would be:

I AM NOW OBTAINING LARGE SUMS OF MONEY BY WINNING LOTTERIES

This sentence is an improvement upon the previous one

because it specifies that the desired outcome is occurring right now, in the present, but it has a new flaw: it is too specific in mentioning exactly how the desire will manifest. It is not good to restrict the channels of manifestation to only lottery winnings, because this is unnecessary, and because it limits the energies of manifestation to only one possibility for receiving money, thus making results more difficult to manifest.

A better statement of this intent would be:

I AM NOW OBTAINING LARGE SUMS OF MONEY BY ANY MEANS THAT ARE TOTALLY ACCEPTABLE TO ME

This sentence is quite acceptable for creating a magical sigil, although it is subject to even further improvement. A good rule of thumb when creating such statements of magical intent is to consider: is there any way that the sentence can be mis-interpreted by anyone to have a meaning different than what you actually desire? For example, using the sentence above, you may very well obtain large sums of money quite rapidly in ways that are legal and totally pleasing to you, but you might not be able to hold on to the money for very long, and your subsequent life experiences may be such that receiving the money doesn't really make you happy or improve your life long-term.

An even better statement of this intent would be:

I AM NOW OBTAINING WEALTH AND PERMANENT FINANCIAL SECURITY IN WAYS THAT ARE TOTALLY ACCEPTABLE FOR ME RIGHT NOW AND INTO THE

FUTURE

With this sentence, you have covered all the bases!

There is one other thing to keep in mind when formulating statements of intent: always phrase the statements using positive language to specify what it is that you desire, and NEVER use negative languaging to specify things that you do NOT want. For example, the sentence

I AM NOT POOR ANYMORE

will virtually guarantee that you'll live in poverty forever, if you use it to create a sigil for manifestation, because the subconscious mind interprets everything in positives and ignores words like No, Not, Never, etc. From the viewpoint of the subconscious, this sentence means "I am poor forever", and that will be the magically manifested intent if this sentence is used to create a sigil.

All intentions must always be phrased positively, like

I AM WEALTHY FOREVER

Keep this in mind when formulating statements of intent.

Creating a Sigil to Symbolize the Intent

Once you have created your statement of intent, the next step is to use this sentence to create a sigil. A sigil is any kind of a symbol that has magical meaning.

Simply use the letters in the statement of intent to create any kind of a symbol ... you can draw the symbol on paper, connecting the letters into a pattern that shares the common lines of each letter. For example, when combining the letters I and T, reduce this to just a T, because the shape of the T includes the shape of the letter I. Similarly, the shape of the letter E includes the shape of the letter F. Combine all the individual letters in the sentence as much as possible, until you have a compact symbol in which all of the letters of the statement are contained. The actual shape of the end result is not important! This shape is your sigil for the statement of intent.

Energizing the Sigil

Engage in any type of sexual activity, either alone or with one or more partners, while visualizing the sigil and meditating upon the desire you wish to manifest. Think about the desire as though it has already occurred in the past, and you simply wish to maintain it for the present and the future.

Anointing the Sigil

When orgasm is achieved, collect all of the ejaculated fluids (either semen alone, vaginal secretions alone, or a mixture of semen and vaginal secretions) and mix them with the saliva of everyone who has participated in this sexual activity ... you may use a small cup to create this mixture. Then, pour this mixture onto the sigils, wetting the paper sigils with it, and then place your mouth close to the sigils and speak the statement of intent onto the sigils, allowing your breath to blow onto the sigils. For sexual activity involving more than one participant, each participant should do this, one at a time.

Storage and Disposal of the Sigil

Store the wet sigil in a plastic bag, and place it in a safe place. You can perform the Energizing and Anointing over and over again until your desire has manifested, at which time you should allow the sigil to air-dry fully, and then burn it using a candle.

Miscellany

Austin Osman Spare was an English artist who is informally recognized as the inventor of modern sigil magic.

Tantric magic has often been viewed as sorcery or witchcraft, and this author will not deny that these attributions are somewhat valid.

Machen, Blackwood, Crowley, Lovecraft, Fortune, and others, frequently used as a theme for their writings the influx of extra-terrestrial powers which have been molding the history of our planet since time began; that is, since time began for us, for we are only too prone to suppose that we were here first and that we alone are here now, whereas the most ancient occult traditions affirm that we were neither the first nor are we the only ones to people the earth; the Great Old Ones and the

Elder Gods find echoes in the myths and legends of all peoples.

Austin Spare claimed to have had direct experience of the existence of extra- terrestrial intelligences, and Crowley- as his autobiography makes abundantly clear- devoted a lifetime to proving that extra-terrestrial and superhuman consciousness can and does exist independently of the human organism.

As explained in Images and Oracles of Austin Osman Spare, Spare was initiated into the vital current of ancient and creative sorcery by an aged woman named Paterson, who claimed decent form a line of Salem witches. The formation of Spare's Cult of the Zos and the Kia owes much to his contact with Witch Paterson who provides the model for many of his 'sabbatic' drawings and paintings. Much of the occult lore that she transmitted to him suffuses two of his books- The Book of Pleasure and the Focus of Life. In the last years of his life he embodied further esoteric researches in a grimoire which he had intended publishing as a sequel to his two other books. Although death prevented its publication, the manuscript survives, and the substance of the grimoire forms the basis of this chapter.

Spare concentrated the theme of his doctrine in the following Affirmation Creed of Zos vel Thanatos.

> I believe in the flesh 'as now' and forever . . . for I am the Light, the Truth, the Law, the Way, and none shall come unto anything except through his flesh. Did I not show you the eclectic path between ecstasies; that precarious funambulatory way . . . . But you had no courage, were tired, and feared. THEN AWAKE! De-hypnotize yourselves from the poor reality you be-live

and be-lie. For the great Noon- tide is here, the great bell has struck . . . Let others await involuntary immolation, the forced redemption so certain for many apostates to Life. Now, in this day, I ask you to search your memories, for great unities are near. The Inceptor of all memory is your Soul. Life is desire, Death is reformation . . . I am the resurrection . . . I, who transcend ecstasy by ecstasy, meditating Need Not Be in Self-love . . .

This creed, informed by the dynamism of Spare's will and his great ability as an artist, created a Cult on the astral plane that attracted to itself all the elements naturally orientated to it. He referred to it as Zos Kia Cultus, and its votaries claimed affinity on the following terms:

Our Sacred Book   : The Book of Pleasure.
Our Path   : The eclectic path between ecstasies; the precarious
                  funambulatory way.
Our Deity   : The All-Prevailing Woman.
                  ('And I strayed with her, into the path direct'.)
Our Creed   : The Living Flesh. (Zos):
                  ('Again I say : This is your great moment of reality- the living flesh').
Our Sacrament   : The Sacred Inbetweenness Concepts.
Our Word   : Does Not Matter-Need Not Be.
Our Eternal Abode   : The mystic state of Neither-Neither.
                  The Atomospheric 'I'. (Kia).
Our Law   : To Trespass all Laws.

The Zos and the Kia are represented by the Hand and the Eye, the instruments of sentiency and vision. They form the foundation of the New Sexuality, which Spare evolved by combining them to form a magical art- the art of visualizing sensation, of 'becoming one with all sensation', and of transcending the dual polarities of existence by the annihilation of separate identity through the mechanics of the Death Posture.[7] Long ago, a Persian poet described in a few words the object of Spare's New Sexuality.

> *The kingdom of I and We forsake, and your home in annihilation make.*

The New Sexuality, in the sense that Spare conceived it, is the sexuality not of positive dualities but of the Great Void, the Negative, the Ain: The Eye of Infinite Potential. The New Sexuality is, simply, the manifestation of non- manifestation, or of Universe 'B', as Bertiaux would have it, which is equivalent to Spare's Neither-Neither concept. Universe 'B' represents the absolute difference of that world of 'all otherness' to anything pertaining to the known world, or Universe 'A'. Its gateway is Daath, sentinelled by the Demon Choronzon. Spare describes this concept as 'the gateway of all inbetweenness'. In terms of Voodoo, this idea is implicit in the Petro rites with their emphasis upon the spaces between the cardinal points of the compass: the off-beat rhythms of the drums that summon the loa from beyond the Veil and formulate the laws of their manifestation. Spare's system of sorcery, as expressed in Zos Kia Cultus, continues in a straight line not only the Petro tradition of Voodoo, but also the Vama Marg of Tantra, with its eight directions of space typified by the Yantra of the Black Goddess, Kali: the Cross of the Four Quarters plus the inbetweenness concepts that together compose the eightfold Cross, the eight-petalled Lotus, a synthetic symbol of the Goddess of the Seven Stars plus her son, Set or Sirius.

The mechanics of the New Sexuality are based upon the dynamics of the Death Posture, a formula evolved by Spare for the purpose of reifying the negative potential in terms of positive power. In ancient Egypt the mummy was the type of this formula, and the simulation by the Adept of the state of death- in Tantric practice- involves also the total stilling of the psychosomatic functions. The formula has been used by Adepts not necessarily working with specifically tantric or magical formulae, notably by the celebrated Advaitin Rishi, Bhagavan Shri Ramana Maharshi of Tiruvannamalai, who attained Supreme Enlightenment by simulating the process of death; and also by the Bengal Vaishnavite, Thakur Haranath, who was taken for dead and actually prepard for burial after a 'death trance' which lasted several hours and from which he emerged with a totally new consciousness that transformed even his bodily constitution and appearance. It is possible that Shri Meher Baba, of Poona, during the period of amnesia that afflicted him in early life, also experienced a form of death from which he emerged with power to enlighten others and to lead a large movement in his name.

The theory of the Death Posture, first described in The Book of Pleasure, was developed independently of the experiences of the above mentioned Masters about whom nothing was published in any European language at that time.

The Rosicrucian mystique of the pastos containing the corpse of Christian Rosencreutz- dramatized by MacGregor Mathers in the 5¡=6ú Ceremony of the Golden Dawn- resumes the mystery of this essentially Egyptian formula of the mummified Osiris. Spare was acquainted with this version of the Mystery. He became a member of Crowley's A.^.A.^., for a brief period, in 1910, and the Golden Dawn rituals- published shortly afterwards in The Equinox may have been available to him.

The concepts of death and sexuality are inextricably connected. Saturn, death, and Venus, life, are twin aspects of the Goddess. That they are, in a mystical sense, one idea is evidenced by the nature of the sexual act. The dynamic activity connected with the drive to know, to penetrate, to illumine, culminates in a stillness, a silence, a cessation of all effort which itsel dissolves in the tranquillity of total negation. The identity of these concepts is explicit in the ancient Chinese equation $0=2$, where naught symbolizes the negative, unmanifest potential of creation, and the two the two polaritites involved in its realization. The Goddess represents the negative phase: the atmospheric 'I' symbolized by that all-seeing Eye with all its ayin symbolism; and the twins- Set-Horus- represent the phase of 2, or duality. The lightning-swift alternations of these terminals, active-passive, are positive emanations of the Void, i.e. the manifestation of the Unmanifest, and the Hand is the symbol of this creative, power-manifesting duality.

The supreme symbol of Zos Kia Cultus therefore resumes that of the Scarlet Woman, and is reminiscent of Crowley's Cult of Love under Will. The Scarlet Woman embodies the Fire Snake, control of which causes 'change to occur in conformity with will'. The energized enthusiasm of the Will is the key to Crowley's Cult, and it is analogous to the technique of magically induced obsession which Spare uses to reify the inherent dream'.

One of the foremost magicians of our time- Salvador Dali- developed a system of magical reification at about the same time that Crowley and Spare were elaborating their doctrines. Dali's system of 'paranoiac-critical activity' evokes echoes of resurgent atavisms that are reflected into the concrete world of images by a process of obsession similar to that induced by the Death Posture.

Dali's birth in 1904- the year in which Crowley received The Book of the Law- makes him, literally, a child of the New Aeon; one of the first! His creative genius adumbrates at every stage of its flight the flowering of the essential germ that has made him a living embodiment of New Aeon consciousness, and of the 'Kingly Man' described in AL.

Dali's objects are reflected in the fluid and ever-shifting luminosity of the Astral Light. They resolve themselves and melt continually into the 'next step', the next phase of consciousness expanding into the further image of Becoming.

Spare had already succeeded in isolating and concentrating desire in a symbol which became sentient and therefore potentially creative through the lightnings of the magnetized will. Dali, it seems, has taken the process a step further. His formula of 'paranoiac-critical activity' is a development of the primal (African) concept of the fetish, and it is instructive to compare Spare's theory of 'visualized sensation' with Dali's definition of painting as 'hand don colour photography of concret irrationality'. Sensation is essentially irrational, and its delineation in graphic form ('hand done colour photography') is identical with Spare's method of 'visualized sensation'.

These magicians utilized human embodiments of power (shakti) which appeared- usually- in feminine form. Each book that Crowley produced had its corresponding shakti. The Rites of Eleusis (1910) were powered, largely, by Leila Waddell. Book Four, Parts I & II (1913) came through Soror Virakam (Mary d'Este). Liber Aleph- The Book of Wisdom or Folly (1918)- was inspired by Soror Hilarion (Jane Foster). His great work, Magick in Theory and Practice, was written mainly in 1920 in Cefalu, where Alostrael (Leah Hirsig) supplied the magical impetus; and so on, up to the New Aeon interpretation of the Tarot (The Book of Thoth), which he produced in collaboration with Frieda Harris in 1944. Dali's shakti- Gala- was the channel through which the inspiring creative current was fixed or visualized in some of the greatest paintings the world has seen. And in the case of Austin Osman Spare, the Fire Snake assumed the form of Mrs. Paterson, a self-confessed witch who embodied the sorceries of a cult so ancient that it was old in Egypt's infancy.

Spare's grimoire is a concentration of the entire body of his work. It comprises, in a sense, everthing of magical or creative value that he ever thought or imagined. Thus, if you posses a picture by Zos, and that picture contains some of his sigillized spells, you possess the whole grimoire, and you stand a great chance of being swept up and attuned to the vibrations of Zos Kia Cultus.

A little known aspect of Spare, an aspect that links up with his friendship with Thomas Burke, reveals the fact that a curious Chinese occult society- known as the Cult of the Ku- flourished in London in the nineteen-twenties. Its headquarters may have been in Peking, Spare did not say, perhaps he did not know; but its London offshoot was not in Limehouse as one might have expected, but in Stockwell, not far from a studio-flat that Spare shared with a friend. A secret session of the cult of the Ku was witnessed by Spare, who seems to have been the only European ever to have gained admittance. He does, in fact, seem to have been the only European apart from Burke who had so much as heard of the Cult. Spare's experience is of exceptional interest by reason of its close approximation to a form of dream-control into which he was initiated many years earlier by Witch Paterson.

The word Ku has several meanings in Chinese, but in this particular case it denotes a peculiar form of sorcery involving elements which Spare had already incorporated in his conception of the New Sexuality. The Adepts of Ku worshipped a serpent goddess in the form of a woman dedicated to the Cult. During an elaborate ritual she would become possessed, with the result that she threw off, or emanated, multiple forms of the goddess as sentient shadows endowed with all the charms possessed by her human representative. These shadow-women, impelled by some subtle law of attraction, gravitated to one or other of the devotees who sat in a drowsy condition around the entranced priestess. Sexual congress with these shadows then occurred and it was the beginning of a sinister form of dream-conrtol involving journeys and encounters in infernal regions.

The Ku would seem to be a form of the Fire Snake exteriorized astrally as a shadow-woman or succubus, congress with which enabled the devotee to reify his 'inherent dream'. She was known as the 'whore of hell' and her function was analogous to that of the Scarlet Woman of Crowley's Cult, the Suvasini of the Tantric Kaula Circle, and the Fiendess of the Cult of the Black Snake. The Chinese Ku, or harlot of hell, is a shadowy embodiment of subconscious desires concentrated in the alluringly sensuous form of the Serpent of Shadow Goddess.

The mechanics of dream control are in many ways similar to those which effect conscious astral projection. My own system of dream control derives from two sources: the formula of Eroto-Comatose Lucidity discovered by Ida Nellidoff and adapted by Crowley to his sex-magical techniques, and Spare's system of Sentient Sigils explained below.

Sleep should be preceded by some form of Karezza during which a specially chosen sigil symbolizing the desired object is vividly visualized. In this manner the libido is baulked of its natural fantasies and seeks satisfaction in the dream world. When the knack is acquired the dream will be extremely intense and dominated by a succube, or shadow-woman, with whom sexual intercourse occurs spontaneously. If the dreamer has aquired even a moderate degree of proficiency in this technique he will be aware of the continued presence of the sigil. This he should bind upon the form of the succube in a place that is within range of his vision during copulation, e.g., as a pendant suspended from her neck; as ear-drops; or as the diadem in a circlet about her brow. Its locus should be determined by the magician with respect to the position he adopts during coitus. The act will then assume all the characteristics of a Ninth Degree Working, because the presence of the Shadow-Woman will be experienced with a vivid intensity of sensation and clarity of vision. The sigil thus becomes sentient and in due course the object of the Working materializes on the physical plane. This object is, of course, determined by the desire embodied in and represented by the sigil.

The important innovation in this system of dream control lies in the transference of the Sigil from the waking to the dream state of consciousness, and the evocation, in the latter state, of the Shadow-woman. This process transforms an Eighth Degree Rite into the similitude of the sexual act as used in Ninth Degree Workings.

Briefly, the formula has three stages:

1. Karezza, or unculminating sexual activity, with visualization of the Sigil until sleep supervenes.

2. Sexual congress in the dream-state with the Shadow-woman evoked by Stage I. The Sigil should appear automatically at this second stage; if it does not, the practice must be repeated at another time. If it does, then the desired result will reify in Stage.

3. after awakening (i.e. in the mundane world of everyday phenomena).

A word of explanation is, perhaps, necessary concerning the term Karezza as used in the present context. Retention of semen is a concept of central importance in certain Tantric practices, the idea being that the bindu (seed) then breeds astrally, not physically. In other words, an entity of some sort is brought to birth at astral levels of consciousness. This, and analogous techniques, have given rise to the impression- quite erroneous- that celibacy is a sine qua non of magical success; but such celibacy is of a purely local character and confined to the physical plane, or waking state, alone. Celibacy, as commonly understood, is therefore a meaningless parody or travesty of the true formula. Such is the initiated rationale of Tantric celibacy, and some such interpretation undoubtedly applies also to other forms of religious asceticism. The 'temptations' of the saints occurred on the astral plane precisely because the physical channels had been deliberately blocked. The state of drowsiness noted in the votaries of the Ku suggests that the ensuing shadow-play was evoked after a fashion similar to that obtained by a species of dream control.

Gerald Massey, Aleister Crowley, Austin Spare, Dion Fortune, have- each in their way- demonstrated the bio-chemical basis of the Mysteries. They achieved in the sphere of the 'occult' that which Wilhelm Reich achieved for psychology, and established it on a sure bio-chemical basis.

Spare's 'sentient symbols' and 'alphabet of desire', correlating as they do the marmas of the body with the specific sex-principles, anticipated in several ways the work of Reich who discovered- between 1936 and 1939- the vehicle of psycho-sexual energy, which he named the orgone. Reich's singular contribution to psychology and, incidentally, to Western occultism, lies in the fact that he successfully isolated the libido and demonstrated its existence as a tangible, biological energy. This energy, the actual substance of Freud's purely hypothetical concepts- libido and id- was measured by Reich, lifted out of the category of hypothesis, and reified. He was, however, wrong in supposing that the orgone was the ultimate energy. It is one of the more important kalas but not the Supreme Kala (Mahakala), although it may become such by virtue of a process not unknown to Tantrics of the Varma Marg. Until comparatively recent times it was known- in the West- to the Arab alchemists, and the entire body of alchemical literature, with its tortuous terminology and hieroglyphic style, reveals- if it reveals anything- a deliberate device on the part of Initiates to veil the true process of distilling the Mahakala.

Reich's discovery is significant because he was probably the first scientist to place psychology on a solid biological basic, ant the first to demonstrate under laboratory conditions the existence of a tangible magical energy at last measurable and therefore strictly scientific. Whether this energy is termed the astral light (Levi), the elan vital (Bergson), the Odic Force (Reichenbach), the libido (Freud), Reich was the first- with the possible exception of Reichenbach- actually to isolate it and demonstrate its properties.

Austin Spare suspected, as early as 1913, that some such energy was the basic factor in the re-activization of primal atavisms, and he treated it accordingly as cosmic energy (the

'Atmospheric I') responsive to subconscious suggestion through the medium of Sentient Symbols, and through the application of the body (Zos) in such a way that it could reify remote atavisms and all possible future forms.

During the time that he was preoccupied with these themes Spare dreamed repeatedly of fantastic buildings whose alignments he found quite impossible to note down on waking. He supposed them to be adumbrations of a future geometry of space-time bearing no known relation to present-day forms of architecture. Eliphaz Levi claimed a similar power of reification for the 'Astral Light', but he failed to show the precise manner of its manipulation. It was to this end that Spare evolved his Alphabet of Desire 'each letter of which relates to a sex-principle'. That is to say he noted certain correspondences between the inner movements of the sexual impulse and the outer form of its manifestation in symbols, sigils, or letters rendered sentient by being charged with its energy. Dali refers to such magically charged fetish-forms as 'accommodations of desire' which are visualized as shadowy voids, black emptinesses, each having the shape of the ghostly object which inhabits its latency, and which IS only by virtue of the fact that it is NOT. This indicates that the origin of manifestation is non-manifestation, and it is plain to intuitive apprehension that the orgone of Reich, the Atmosheric 'I' of Austin Spare, and the Dalinian delineations of the 'accommodations of desire' refer in each case to an identical Energy manifesting through the mechanics of desire. Desire, Energized Will, and Obsession, are the keys to unlimited manifestation, for all form and all power is latent in the Void, and its god-form is the Death Posture.

These theories have their roots in very ancient practices, some of which- in distorted form- provided the basis of the medieval Witch Cult, covens of which flourished in New England at the time of the Salem Witch Trials at the end of the 17th century. The subsequent persecutions apparently obliterated all outer manifestations both of the genuine cult and its debased counterfeits.

The principal symbols of the original cult have survived the passage of aeon- long cycles of time. They all suggest the Backward Way: The Sabbath sacred to Sevekh or Sebt, the number Seven, the Moon, the Cat, Jackal, Hyaena, Pig, Black Snake, and other animals considered unclean by later traditions; the Widdershins and Back-to-Back dance, the Anal Kiss, the number Thirteen, the Witch mounted on the besom handle, the Bat, and other forms of webbed or winged nocturnal creature; the Batrachia generally, of which the Toad, Frog, or Hekt was preeminent. These and similar symbols originally typified the Draconian Tradition which was degraded by the pseudo witch-cults during centuries of Christian persecution. The Mysteries were profaned and the sacred rites were condemned as anti-Christian. The Cult thus became the repository of inverted and perverted religious rites and symbols having no inner meaning; mere affirmations of the witches' total commitment to anti-Christian doctrine whereas- originally- they were living emblems, sentient symbols, of ante- Christian faith.

Astrological Considerations

When attempting to manifest desires that involve increases in things like money, love, opportunities, health, knowledge, personal power, spiritual advancement, etc., it is best to perform the magical rituals a few hours before a Full moon. To manifest desires that involve decreases in things like sickness, problems, and unwanted circumstances, it is best to perform the magical rituals a few hours before a New moon. Most newspapers publish the dates for the current lunar cycle in the section that provides information on local weather, sunrise and sunset times, and ocean tides.

If you have studied astrology or planetary magic, then you can elect very precise dates and exact times at which to perform your rituals, using electional astrology and modern astrological computer software.

References

1). http://www.666blacksun.com/Sexual_Freedom.htm

2). http://gblt.webs.com/index.htm

3). http://www.tantricjoy.com

4). http://redtantra.com

5). http://www.astro.com

Made in the USA
Middletown, DE
31 May 2019